1997 I

Suggested Solutions

Commercial Law

LLB

University of London
External Examinations
Solutions by Pamela Sellman
LLM (London), MA (Business Law),
Barrister, Attorney (New York)

HLT Publications

HLT PUBLICATIONS
200 Greyhound Road, London W14 9RY

Reprinted 2000

ISBN 0 7510 0836 2

British Library Cataloguing-in-Publication.

A CIP Catalogue record for this book is available from the British Library.

Printed and bound in Great Britain.

CONTENTS

ACKNOWLEDGEMENT

The questions used are taken from the University of London LLB (External) Degree examination paper and our thanks are extended to the University of London for the kind permission which has been given to us to use and publish the questions.

Caveat

The answers given are not approved or sanctioned by the University of London and are entirely our responsibility.

They are not intended as 'Model Answers', but rather as Suggested Solutions.

The answers have two fundamental purposes, namely:

a) To provide a detailed example of a suggested solution to examination questions, and

b) To assist students with their research into the subject and to further their understanding and appreciation of the subject.

Note

Please note that the solutions in this book were written in the year of the examination. They were appropriate solutions at the time of preparation, but students must note that certain caselaw and statutes may subsequently have changed.

INTRODUCTION

Why choose HLT publications?

Holborn College has earned an international reputation for the outstanding quality of its teaching, Textbooks, Casebooks and Suggested Solutions to past examination papers.

Our expertise is reflected in the outstanding results achieved by our students in the examinations conducted by the University of London LLB Honours Degree Programme for External Students, the Council of Legal Education, and by students in over 70 universities who use our publications.

Suggested Solutions

The Suggested Solutions series provides examples of full answers to the problems posed by examiners. The solutions are much more than answers achievable by a candidate under examination conditions. The opportunity has been taken, where appropriate, to develop themes, suggest alternatives and set out additional material providing further comprehensive topical coverage.

To aid comprehension and revision, the solutions are fuller than would be possible under examination conditions. It is important to keep in mind that at this level there almost certainly is more than just one approach in answering any given question.

We feel that in writing full opinion answers we can assist you with your research and further your understanding and appreciation of the law.

Notes on examination technique

Although the SUBSTANCE and SLANT of the answer changes according to the subject-matter of the question, the examining body and syllabus concerned, the TECHNIQUE of answering examination questions does not change.

You will not pass an examination if you do not know the substance of a course. You may pass if you do not know how to go about answering a question although this is doubtful. To do well and to guarantee success, however, it is necessary to learn the technique of answering problems properly. The following is a guide to acquiring that technique.

Time

All examinations permit only a limited time for papers to be completed. All papers require you to answer a certain number of questions in that time, and the questions, with some exceptions carry equal marks.

It follows from this that you should never spend a disproportionate amount of time on any question. When you have used up the amount of time allowed for any one question STOP and go on to the next question after an abrupt conclusion, if necessary. If you feel that you are running out of time, then complete your answer in note form. A useful way of ensuring that you do not over-run is to write down on a piece of scrap paper the time at which you should be starting each part of the paper. This can be done in the few minutes before the examination begins and it will help you to calm any nerves you may have.

Reading the question

It will not be often that you will be able to answer every question on an examination paper. Inevitably, there will be some areas in which you feel better prepared than others. You will prefer to answer the questions which deal with those areas, but you will never know how good the questions are unless you read the whole examination paper.

You should spend at least 10 MINUTES at the beginning of the examination reading the questions. Preferably, you should read them more than once. As you go through each question, make a brief note on the examination paper of any relevant cases and/or statutes that occur to you even if you think you may not answer that question: you may well be grateful for this note towards the end of the examination when you are tired and your memory begins to fail.

Re-reading the answers

Ideally, you should allow time to re-read your answers. This is rarely a pleasant process, but will ensure that you do not make any silly mistakes such as leaving out a 'not' when the negative is vital.

The structure of the answer

Almost all examination problems raise more than one legal issue that you are required to deal with. Your answer should:

Identify the issues raised by the question

This is of crucial importance and gives shape to the whole answer. It indicates to the examiner that you appreciate what he is asking you about.

This is at least as important as actually answering the questions of law raised by that issue.

The issues should be identified in the first paragraph of the answer.

Deal with those issues one by one as they arise in the course of the problem

This, of course, is the substance of the answer and where study and revision pays off.

If the answer to an issue turns on a provision of a statute, CITE that provision briefly, but do not quote it from any statute you may be permitted to bring into the examination hall

Having cited the provision, show how it is relevant to the question.

If there is no statute, or the meaning of the statute has been interpreted by the courts, CITE the relevant cases

'Citing cases' does not mean writing down the name of every case that happens to deal with the general topic with which you are concerned and then detailing all the facts you can think of.

You should cite only the most relevant cases – there may perhaps only be one. No more facts should be stated than are absolutely essential to establish the relevance of the case. If there is a relevant case, but you cannot remember its name, it is sufficient to refer to it as 'one decided case'.

Whenever a statute or case is cited, the title of statute or the name of the case should be underlined

This makes the examiner's job much easier because he can see at a glance whether the relevant material has been dealt with, and it will make him more disposed in your favour.

Having dealt with the relevant issues, summarise your conclusions in such a way that you answer the question

A question will often say at the end simply 'Advise A', or B, or C, etc. The advice will usually turn on the individual answers to a number of issues. The point made here is that the final paragraph should pull those individual answers together and actually give the advice required. For example, it may begin something like: 'The effect of the answer to the issues raised by this question is that one's advice to A is that ...'

Related to the previous paragraph, make sure at the end that you have answered the question

For example, if the question says 'Advise A', make sure that is what your answer does. If you are required to advise more than one party, make sure that you have dealt with all the parties that you are required to and no more.

Some general points

You should always try to get the examiner on your side. One method has already been mentioned – the underlining of case names, etc. There are also other ways as well.

Always write as neatly as you can. This is more easily done with ink than with a ball-point.

Avoid the use of violently coloured ink, eg turquoise; this makes a paper difficult to read.

Space out your answers sensibly: leave a line between paragraphs. You can always get more paper. At the same time, try not to use so much paper that your answer book looks too formidable to mark. This is a question of personal judgment.

NEVER put in irrelevant material simply to show that you are clever. Irrelevance is not a virtue and time spent on it is time lost for other, relevant, answers.

EXAMINATION PAPER

UNIVERSITY OF LONDON
LLB EXAMINATIONS 1997
for External Students
PARTS I & II EXAMINATIONS (Scheme A)
THIRD AND FOURTH YEAR EXAMINATIONS (Scheme B)
GRADUATE ENTRY LEVEL II (Route A)
GRADUATE ENTRY THIRD YEAR EXAMINATIONS (Route B)

COMMERCIAL LAW

Friday, 13 June: 10.00 am to 1.00 pm

Answer *FOUR* of the following EIGHT questions.

(Assume that all contracts are governed by English law)

1 Able agreed to buy a car from Bad Garage Ltd. The agreed price was £16,000 but Bad agreed to accept Able's car in part exchange. It was valued at £1,500. Able asked Bad Garage Ltd if they could arrange to finance the balance. Bad Garage Ltd agreed to make the necessary arrangements. Bad Garage Ltd sent to Able's house a hire-purchase proposal form which involved an agreement with Credit Angel Ltd with whom Bad Garage had an arrangement. Able filled in the details required by the proposal form and sent it to Bad Garage Ltd who forwarded it to Credit Angel Ltd. The manager of Credit Angel Ltd signed the agreement (sending a copy to Able) and paid Bad Garage Ltd for the car. Able collected the car and two weeks later, when Able had made two of the thirty-six payments, the car's engine blew up. The car was towed to Bad Garage Ltd and the repairs were estimated at £2,000. Able wrote to Bad Garage Ltd saying, 'I no longer want this car and I want my money back.' Able refused to collect the car, pay for the repair or pay any more instalments.

Advise Able. What difference, if any, would it make to your advice if, (a) when Bad Garage Ltd had sent the proposal form it had been signed first by Credit Angel Ltd and was accompanied by a copy of the document; and, alternatively, (b) the proposal document and copies contained notice of the right to cancel?

2 'The subject of description in sale of goods law would never win any accolades for clarity of definition.' (Bridge)

Critically evaluate this statement and consider, in particular, any improvements which could be made to the drafting of section 13 of the Sale of Goods Act 1979.

3 'As any student of agency law will tell you, the doctrine of the undisclosed principal is a tricky and unpredictable one, embodying as it does a volatile cocktail of legal anomaly and commercial expediency.' (Tettenborn)

Critically evaluate this statement.

4 a) Critically evaluate the approach which the courts have adopted towards the interpretation of time stipulations in fob and cif contracts.

b) Why are the doctrines of strict compliance and autonomy of the credit of such great importance in the law relating to letters of credit? What is the juridical basis of these doctrines?

5 BSH plc are suppliers of office equipment. They have recently encountered a number of problems with customers in connection with the following contracts and they seek your advice.

a) BSH sold a computer to Jack, a self-employed accountant, who bought the computer both for use in his business and for use by his children. The screen of the computer has a thin scratch running across it but the scratch does not affect the operation of the computer in any way. Jack claims that he is entitled to reject the computer. The price of the computer has dropped sharply on the market.

b) BSH supplied two chairs to Susan, a self-employed estate agent. Susan claims that the fabric on the back of the chair has caused her to contract a rare skin infection and she has now been off work for a number of weeks. The other chair was used by Anne, a secretary whom Susan employed on a part-time basis. Last week the chair suddenly gave way when Anne was sitting on it and Anne suffered extensive injuries in the fall.

c) BSH sold a photocopier to Xerxes plc. The contract stated that:

> 'To remedy defects the purchaser shall allow the supplier the time and opportunity required as estimated by the supplier. Should the purchaser refuse to allow such time and opportunity, the supplier shall be released from the obligations to remedy the defects. The purchaser shall return the defective goods at his own expense to the supplier immediately upon request of the latter. All other warranties or conditions are hereby expressly excluded.'

Yugo, the managing director of Xerxes, claims that the photocopier is defective but he refuses to return the photocopier for repair because he claims that a local supplier can carry out the repairs effectively and he wishes to recover the cost of repair from BSH. Alternatively, he claims that, if he is obliged by the terms of the contract to return the goods to BSH, Xerxes cannot be made to pay for the cost of returning the photocopier to BSH.

6 a) Albert has 1,000 bottles of wine in his warehouse. He agreed to sell 200 bottles each to Brian, Cedric, Donald and Evelina and 100 bottles each to Frank and Gerald. All but Gerald paid Albert in advance. Under the terms of the contracts of sale Albert agreed to supply the stipulated quantities of wine from his warehouse, but he reserved the right to supply wine of the same quality from another source in the event of a shortfall for whatever reason of the stocks in his warehouse. Albert is now insolvent but he has not supplied any of his purchasers with their wine.

Advise the purchasers. What difference would it make to your answer if Frank, Brian and Cedric had taken delivery of their wine prior to the insolvency of Albert and it is now discovered that there are only 300 bottles of wine in the warehouse?

b) Pablo, a Spanish wine merchant, agreed to sell 5,000 bottles of sherry to Albert fob Bilbao. Pablo entered into a contract with Picasso Ltd for the carriage of the sherry on board the vessel *Enterprise*. After the sherry had been loaded onto the *Enterprise*, but before it reaches London, Pablo is told that Albert is bankrupt and that he will not be able to pay for the goods. He has also been told that some of the sherry has been damaged as a result of being stowed on deck rather than below deck. The contract of carriage was silent on the point whether the goods must be stowed above deck or below deck.

Advise Pablo.

7 a) Critically evaluate section 24 of the Sale of Goods Act 1979. Should the section be reformed? If so, how?

b) Lotty Leather plc entered into a contract with Sharp Shoes Ltd under which Lotty agreed to supply Sharp with 'all its requirements for leather in the manufacture of shoes'. A further term of the contract stated that ownership of the leather was to remain with Lotty until payment had been made in full under all orders. While Sharp were given authority to sell any goods which had been made with leather supplied by Lotty, they could only do so if they entered into any such sales contracts as agents for Lotty and they paid all the proceeds of sale over to Lotty without delay. Sharp is now insolvent. Leather to the value of £7,000 has been found in Sharp's factory. Some of the leather has been cut. There are also shoes worth £12,000 in the factory and Sharp has entered into a number of contracts 'as agent for Lotty Leather' under which the customers remain liable to pay £12,000. Sharp owe Lotty Leather £30,000.

Advise Lotty Leather.

8 Martin is the manager of the Red Dwarf Hotel. The hotel is owned by Crust plc. It is a term of Martin's contract that he must not, without the authority of the managing director of Crust, place an order for goods worth more than £10,000. Martin is also expressly forbidden from ordering any alcohol because all alcohol is supplied to the hotel directly by Crust. Nora, a sales representative of Prosper Foods, visits Martin and persuades him that it makes good business sense to order his food in bulk and that Prosper has special discounts on all orders over £15,000. Martin informs Nora that he needs the authority of his managing director to place an order in excess of £10,000. While Nora is in his office, Martin picks up the phone and pretends to hold a conversation with his managing director in which he appears to obtain the permission of his managing director to enter into the transaction (in fact he was talking to his girlfriend, Roberta). Martin then signs a contract to order food to the value of £17,000 in his own name. Nora also persuades Martin to enter into a contract to purchase £5,000 worth of alcohol by offering to give him 100 free cigars.

The hotel is rather run down and requires redecoration. Martin has received from a local firm a quotation of £12,000 for the work. He decides that his two brothers could do the job more cheaply. They work for a small company, of which Martin is also a director. Martin enters into an agreement with his brother under which he agrees to pay them £9,800 and to provide them and their families with free meals for a year if they carry out the redecoration work. They agree. The redecoration has now been done and Prosper has delivered the food and alcohol to the Red Dwarf Hotel. The managing director of Crust, having discovered the above facts, is refusing to pay either Martin's brothers or Prosper and is threatening to dismiss Martin.

Discuss.

SUGGESTED SOLUTIONS

QUESTION 1

Able agreed to buy a car from Bad Garage Ltd. The agreed price was £16,000 but Bad agreed to accept Able's car in part exchange. It was valued at £1,500. Able asked Bad Garage Ltd if they could arrange to finance the balance. Bad Garage Ltd agreed to make the necessary arrangements. Bad Garage Ltd sent to Able's house a hire-purchase proposal form which involved an agreement with Credit Angel Ltd with whom Bad Garage had an arrangement. Able filled in the details required by the proposal form and sent it to Bad Garage Ltd who forwarded it to Credit Angel Ltd. The manager of Credit Angel Ltd signed the agreement (sending a copy to Able) and paid Bad Garage Ltd for the car. Able collected the car and two weeks later, when Able had made two of the thirty-six payments, the car's engine blew up. The car was towed to Bad Garage Ltd and the repairs were estimated at £2,000. Able wrote to Bad Garage Ltd saying, 'I no longer want this car and I want my money back.' Able refused to collect the car, pay for the repair or pay any more instalments.

Advise Able. What difference, if any, would it make to your advice if, (a) when Bad Garage Ltd had sent the proposal form it had been signed first by Credit Angel Ltd and was accompanied by a copy of the document; and, alternatively, (b) the proposal document and copies contained notice of the right to cancel?

SUGGESTED SOLUTION TO QUESTION 1

General Comment

This is a fairly straightforward question dealing with a hire-purchase agreement. It raises the issue of the debtor's right to cancel, withdraw or terminate an agreement. The answer should involve a discussion of the defect in the car and s10 Supply of Goods (Implied Terms) Act 1973.

Skeleton Solution

HP agreement: s12(a) Consumer Credit Act 1974.

Formalities.

Cancellable agreement: s67 Consumer Credit Act 1974.

Notice of cancellation rights: s64 Consumer Credit Act 1974.

Misrepresentation: s56 Consumer Credit Act 1974.

Section 10 Supply of Goods (Implied Terms) Act 1973.

Suggested Solution

The hire-purchase agreement that Able has entered into is a regulated agreement within the meaning of the Consumer Credit Act (CCA) 1974. It is a personal agreement for credit below £15,000 and it is not exempt under s16 CCA 1974. The agreement is a two-party Debtor-Creditor-Supplier agreement: s12(a) CCA 1974. Bad Garage Ltd, the dealer, is deemed to be the agent of the creditor, Credit Angel Ltd, for the purpose of any antecedent negotiations: s56 CCA 1974.

Assuming Bad Garage Ltd made oral representations to Able during the negotiations, the agreement is a cancellable agreement as Able signed the agreement at home: s67 CCA 1974. The oral representations must amount to a statement 'of fact or opinion or an undertaking as to the future which was capable of inducing the proposed borrower to enter the agreement' (per Staughton LJ in *Moorgate Services Ltd* v *Kabir* (1)).

On signing the agreement Able should have been given a copy of the unexecuted agreement (s62 CCA 1974) and a copy of the executed agreement within seven days of the making of the agreement: s63 CCA 1974. We are told that Able received a copy of the agreement after Credit Angel Ltd had signed it, but it is unclear as to whether the copy contained notice of Able's cancellation rights as required under s64 CCA 1974. If the copy did not contain such a notice, the agreement is indefinitely cancellable. The court shall not make an enforcement order against the debtor: s127(4) CCA 1974.

On the assumption that the copy did not contain a notice of cancellation rights and, therefore, Able is not restricted by a cooling-off period, Able was in effect cancelling the agreement when he sent the letter to Bad Garage Ltd. The notice of cancellation which must be in writing may be sent to the dealer as agent of the creditor: s69 CCA 1974.

On cancellation the goods must be made available for the creditor and any money paid by the debtor must be returned by the person to whom it was paid: ss72 and 70 respectively. The car is in fact in the possession of Bad Garage Ltd who has carried out the repairs. Under the hire-purchase agreement the owner of the car is Credit Angel Ltd, who will recover the car from Bad Garage Ltd subject to the latter's lien for the cost of repairs.

Able would have a claim against Credit Angel Ltd for the return of the money and, possibly, a claim in damages for misrepresentation. Any misrepresentation made by Bad Garage Ltd during negotiations would be made by them in their own capacity as well as agent of Credit Angel Ltd: s56 CCA 1974. Alternatively, Able may have a claim against Bad Garage Ltd based on a breach of a collateral contract: *Andrews* v *Hopkinson* (2).

The car's engine blew up two weeks after Able collected the car from Bad Garage Ltd. There is an implied term in a hire-purchase agreement that the goods supplied shall be of satisfactory quality and fit for their purpose: s10 Supply of Goods (Implied Terms) Act (SG(IT)A) 1973. The definition of satisfactory quality is the same as for Sale of Goods Act 1979, ie the standard that a reasonable person would regard as satisfactory taking into account the description, price (if relevant) and other relevant circumstances. Cases to date have dealt with the test of merchantable quality, and certainly goods which are not of merchantable quality would not be of satisfactory quality. There have been numerous cases dealing with cars, such as *Bernstein* v *Pamson Motors (Golders Green) Ltd* (3) and *Shine* v *General Guarantee Corporation Ltd* (4), which would support Able's claim there had been a breach of s10 SG(IT)A 1973.

However, Able's right to reject the car would be lost if he has affirmed the contract. In *Farnworth Finance Facilities* v *Attryde* (5) it was held that affirmation means electing to go on with the contract despite the defects. As Able wrote to Bad Garage Ltd immediately after the car's engine blew up, it is unlikely that he has affirmed the contract.

a) If, when Able signed the agreement it had first been signed by Credit Angel Ltd, Able's signature would have turned the agreement into an executed agreement. The effect would be that once executed it would be too late for Able to withdraw from the hire-purchase agreement.

   Until an agreement is executed a debtor may withdraw from the agreement even if it is not a cancellable agreement: s57(4) CCA 1974. The withdrawal notice, whether oral or in writing, must be communicated to the offeror, ie Credit Angel Ltd. Notice to Bad Garage Ltd would be an effective notice of withdrawal: *Dickinson* v *Dodds* (6).

b) If the copy of the agreement received by Able had contained a notice of cancellation rights, Able would have had a cooling-off period of five days following the day of receipt of the notice: s68 CCA 1974. We are told that two weeks after receiving the copy of the executed agreement Able wrote to Bad Garage Ltd demanding the return of his money. Able's notice of cancellation would have been outside the five days' cooling-off period and Able would, therefore, be unable to cancel the hire-purchase agreement. In which case, the letter sent by Able to Bad Garage Ltd may be construed as terminating the agreement.

A debtor has the right at any time before final payment to terminate a regulated hire-purchase agreement: s99 CCA 1974. If Able did terminate the agreement he would not be entitled to the return of the money he had already paid under the agreement.

Credit Angel Ltd would be entitled to arrears of instalments. If the agreement contains a clause to the effect that on termination Able is required to make a further payment, that sum will be limited to an amount which would bring payments made up to one-half of the total price: s100 CCA 1974.

Alternatively, it could be argued that Able did not terminate the agreement but that in fact he had committed a breach of the agreement. If there is a breach of the agreement, Credit Angel Ltd would be entitled to bring a claim in damages against Able: *Overstone* v *Shipway* (7). The measure of damages may work out to be less than the amount required to be paid under a termination clause. In such a case the court may construe Able's conduct as a breach of the agreement because this would result in less of a financial burden on Able: *Bridge* v *Campbell Discount Co Ltd* (8).

References

(1) [1995] CCLR 74
(2) [1957] 1 QB 229
(3) [1987] 2 All ER 220
(4) [1988] 1 All ER 911
(5) [1970] 1 WLR 1053
(6) (1876) 2 Ch D 463
(7) [1962] 1 WLR 117
(8) [1962] AC 600

QUESTION 2

'The subject of description in sale of goods law would never win any accolades for clarity of definition.' (Bridge)

Critically evaluate this statement and consider, in particular, any improvements which could be made to the drafting of section 13 of the Sale of Goods Act 1979.

SUGGESTED SOLUTION TO QUESTION 2

General Comment

There are many cases dealing with description under s13 Sale of Goods Act 1979. However, students would encounter problems in answering the question if their knowledge was confined to the facts and not the legal principles raised in those cases.

Skeleton Solution

Section 13 Sale of Goods Act 1979.

Definition.

Specific v unascertained goods.

Words of description v words of inducement.

Reliance.

Breach of conditions.

Possible reform?

Suggested Solution

Section 13 Sale of Goods Act (SGA) 1979 provides that where there is a contract of sale by description, it is an implied condition that the goods supplied shall correspond with that description. Section 13(3) SGA 1979 states that even if the buyer selects the goods, the sale may still be one by description. Problems have arisen in trying to define when a contract is one by description and what actually amounts to words of description.

In *Varley* v *Whipp* (1), where the buyer of a reaping machine did not see it until delivery, but had relied on the description, it was held that it was a case which came within the term 'sale of goods by description'. Although the term would usually be applied to the sale of unascertained goods, it could also apply to the sale of the reaping machine where there was no identification otherwise than by description. This case is, therefore, applying the term 'sale by description' to the sale of a specific good. Professor Roy Goode (*Commercial Law,* 2nd ed) argues that the word 'description' changes meaning when applied to specific goods.

When used in connection with specific goods the term 'description' does not identify the article but instead identifies the essential characteristics which the article must possess. If the specific goods fail to possess the characteristics which are deemed essential to the performance of the obligation by the seller, the buyer may reject the goods. Yet, because the goods were still unique to the contract, the seller would not have the right to cure the breach by tendering other goods (Goode, *Commercial Law,* 2nd ed, p309). The phrase 'sale by description' is, therefore, being used in a different way when applied to specific goods. Whereas when applied to unascertained goods, 'sale by description' identifies the subject-matter of the contract of sale.

It is important to distinguish between words of description and words which form the basis of a collateral warranty: *Varley* v *Whipp*. In *Heilbut, Symons & Co* v *Buckleton* (2) the House of Lords held that words of description which become a term of the contract must be distinguished from words of inducement which encourage someone to enter into the contract of sale. In *Ashington Piggeries Ltd* v *Christopher Hill Ltd* (3), Lord Wilberforce stressed the need for the test of description to be applied using common sense and in the context of the mercantile market. In that case the herring meal which was contaminated could still be described as herring meal and, therefore, there was no breach of description. However, the addition of a foreign element could change the identity of the goods. In *Robert A Munro & Co Ltd* v *Meyer* (4), meat and bone meal which was found to contain cocoa husks was no longer identifiable as meat and bone meal.

The words of description must be relied on by the buyer. In *Harlingdon & Leinster Enterprises Ltd* v *Christopher Hull Fine Art* (5), where the buyer purchased two paintings described as being painted by a particular artist, it was held that the buyer had not relied on the description. The buyer examined the paintings and was more of an expert than the seller, hence the description was not a term of the contract, a breach of which would entitle the buyer to reject the paintings.

Discussions have sometimes centred around whether a breach of s13 SGA 1979 should be seen as a breach of warranty rather than a breach of condition: *Reardon Smith Line Ltd* v *Hansen-Tangen* (6). However, decisions such as those in *Arcos Ltd* v *A E Ronaasen & Son* (7) and *Re Moore & Co Ltd and Landauer & Co* (8) suggest that a breach of s13 would always be a breach of condition. In *Arcos Ltd* the House of Lords held that the buyer was entitled to reject a consignment of staves when it was found that they were not of the correct thickness. The goods were still merchantable but it was stated that if the seller wanted a margin that should be inserted into the contract.

In *Re Moore,* despite the fact that the overall amount of goods delivered was correct, the buyer was entitled to reject the goods when they were delivered in cases each containing 24 tins instead of the required 30 tins.

It would, therefore, appear that even if the buyer has not suffered loss by the breach of s13 SGA 1979, he/she may still reject the goods. However, this is now, of course, subject to s15A SGA 1979. Section 15A in turn causes problems. When is a breach so slight that it is unreasonable to reject?

In conclusion, it is certainly true that the subject of description in sale of goods law does not give rise to a clear definition. Some of the problems occur because 'description' has been given such a wide interpretation. It covers such things as: the method of packing (*Re Moore*); the time of shipment (*Bowes & Co* v *Shand & Co* (9)); and the thickness of staves (*Arcos* v *Ronaasen*). It is not always easy to identify the words which form an essential part of the description of the goods: *Reardon Smith Line Ltd* v *Hansen-Tangen*.

Some of the problems could be dealt with by amendments to the legislation. However, one wonders whether any type of statutory definition would be able to cover the vast array of cases which come before the courts. Perhaps in the words of Lord Wilberforce (10):

> 'The test of description, at least where commodities are concerned, is intended to be a broader, more commonsense, test of a mercantile character. The question whether that is what the buyer bargained for has to be answered according to such tests as men in the market would apply ...'.

References

(1) [1900] 1 QB 513
(2) [1913] AC 30
(3) [1972] AC 441
(4) [1930] 2 KB 312
(5) [1991] 1 QB 564
(6) [1976] 1 WLR 989
(7) [1933] AC 470
(8) [1921] 2 KB 159
(9) (1877) 2 App Cas 455
(10) *Ashington Piggeries Ltd* v *Christopher Hill Ltd* [1972] AC 441 at 489

QUESTION 3

'As any student of agency law will tell you, the doctrine of the undisclosed principal is a tricky and unpredictable one, embodying as it does a volatile cocktail of legal anomaly and commercial expediency.' (Tettenborn)

Critically evaluate this statement.

SUGGESTED SOLUTION TO QUESTION 3

General Comment

A question requiring discussion of the problems of the doctrine of the undisclosed principal. There are a number of cases on this area, but students should select those cases supporting the points they wish to make.

Skeleton Solution

Definition of doctrine.

Criteria: agent's description; personality of the parties.

Is the doctrine unpredictable?

Does the doctrine embody commercial expediency?

Suggested Solution

The doctrine of the undisclosed principal arises when an agent has not disclosed the fact of the agency when entering into a contract with a third party. The third party is, therefore, unaware of the identity, or even the existence, of the principal. Yet, despite this fact, the doctrine of the undisclosed principal allows the principal to intervene and to enforce the contract against the third party. This exception to the privity of contract principle is peculiar to English law.

The doctrine of the undisclosed principal, which has developed over the years, is subject to certain criteria. Since the third party is unaware of the existence of the principal, there is no issue of apparent authority. The undisclosed principal may only step in and enforce the contract if the agent has acted within his/her actual authority. Furthermore, the agent must appear to be acting as principal in the contract entered into with the third party, but the agent must not have actually denied the existence of an agency. If the agent does in fact deny that there is an agency, the undisclosed principal will not be able to step in and the third party may enforce the contract against the agent.

Unfortunately, it is not always easy to predict when the above criteria for the undisclosed principal doctrine have been met. For example, it is not always clear when an agent is actually denying the existence of an agency. The courts have sometimes resorted to looking at how the agent has signed the contract. In *Fred Drughorn Ltd* v *Rederiaktiebolaget Transatlantic* (1) an agent signed a contract for the hire of a ship as 'charterer'. It was held that the description 'charterer' was not inconsistent with there being an agency. Whereas in *Humble* v *Hunter* (2) it was held that to sign as 'owner' was in fact an assertion that an agency did not exist. These two cases may appear to be easy to reconcile, but there will be many descriptions which are not readily definable. For instance, in *Epps* v *Rothnie* (3), an agent described himself as 'landlord' and it was held that this description was not inconsistent with the existence of an agency. If the test is 'how would the statement be interpreted by a reasonable person?', it is questionable whether the description 'landlord' does not in fact lead a third party to believe that there is no agency and the agent is in fact the owner of the property. In *Siu (Yin Kwan)* v *Eastern Insurance Co* (4) the Privy Council held that for an agent to be described as 'the insured' in an insurance contract did not preclude the existence of an agency.

The undisclosed principal will not be able to step into the contract where the identity of the agent is vital to the contract and the third party believes that he/she is making a contract with the agent as principal. In *Said* v *Butt* (5) it was held that the personality of the parties was important, and the undisclosed principal could not use the theatre ticket which had been purchased by the agent from the third party, the theatre owner. This was because the theatre owner would not have sold a ticket to the principal. In *Dyster* v *Randall & Sons* (6) the personalities of the parties were not considered vital to the contract and the undisclosed principal was allowed to intervene and enforce a contract for the sale of land. The two cases can be reconciled on the basis that the sale of land is seen as an impersonal contract, in that the vendor will usually sell to anyone who meets the asking price, but it is not always clear when the courts will find a personal element in the contract. In *Siu (Yin Kwan)* v *Eastern Insurance Co*, the Privy Council rejected the argument that an insurance contract was a personal contract and, therefore, an undisclosed principal could intervene despite the fact that the agent had described himself as 'the insured' and the policy was not assignable.

The doctrine of the undisclosed principal may well be considered a legal anomaly as it allows a previously unidentified person to step into a contract which the third party has entered into unaware of the existence of an agency. Once the undisclosed principal has stepped in, he/she may sue and be sued on the contract. The cases on this area illustrate that it is not always easy to predict when the courts will allow the undisclosed principal to intervene, although cases such as *Siu (Yin Kwan)* v *Eastern Insurance Co* suggest that the courts will use the doctrine of the undisclosed principal for commercial expediency.

References

(1) [1919] AC 203
(2) (1848) 12 QB 310
(3) [1945] KB 562
(4) [1994] 1 All ER 213
(5) [1920] 3 KB 497
(6) [1926] Ch 932

QUESTION 4

a) Critically evaluate the approach which the courts have adopted towards the interpretation of time stipulations in fob and cif contracts.

b) Why are the doctrines of strict compliance and autonomy of the credit of such great importance in the law relating to letters of credit? What is the juridical basis of these doctrines?

SUGGESTED SOLUTION TO QUESTION 4

General Comment

This is a straightforward question on the export sales part of the syllabus. Candidates should be able to score well, provided they resisted the tendency to write 'an everything you know' answer.

Skeleton Solution

a) Time stipulation in commercial contracts.
   Date of loading and notice of loading.
   Shipment period as part of description.
   Reasonable time.

b) Doctrine of strict compliance:
      documents;
      bank's duty of care;
      UCP: arts 13 and 15.
   Autonomy of credit:
      guarantee of payment;
      UCP: arts 3 and 4;
      fraud by beneficiary exception.

Suggested Solution

a) Time stipulations relate to various stages in the fob and cif contracts. As both of these contracts are commercial contracts, time is usually of the essence: *Bunge Corporation* v *Tradax Export SA* (1).

   In both fob and cif contracts there will be a contractual shipment period, ie the period in which the goods must be loaded. The shipment date is the date when loading is completed. In the cif contract the seller has the benefit of the shipment period in that he/she will decide on what date within the shipment period loading is to take place. The fob contract has three main variants: *Pyrene Co Ltd* v *Scindia Navigation Co Ltd* (2). Under the three main types of fob contract, often labelled as strict, classic and fob with additional or extended services, the party who is arranging carriage will usually be the one who nominates the date of shipment.

   In the strict fob contract it is the buyer who nominates the date of loading and he/she will give the seller a notice of loading, ie informing the seller when to have the goods at port ready for shipment. The contract will usually include a clause whereby the buyer must give the seller the notice of loading within so many days prior to the date of shipment. If the buyer fails to comply with the notice period, the seller does not have to perform his/her obligations under the contract and will, in fact, be able to cancel the contract due to the buyer's repudiatory breach and claim damages: *Bunge & Co Ltd* v *Tradax England Ltd* (3).

Under both the fob and cif contracts the seller must complete loading by the end of the shipment period, and failure to do so will entitle the buyer to cancel the contract. This is, of course, subject to the buyer having made an effective nomination of a ship under the fob contract: *Yelo* v *San Machado* (4). If, under the fob contract, a substitute vessel may be nominated the buyer must ensure that the substitution still allows the seller to complete loading within the stipulated time: *Agricultores Federados Argentinos* v *Ampro SA* (5).

In both fob and cif contracts early or late shipment will be a repudiatory breach of the contract, as the shipment date/period is part of the description of the goods: *Bowes & Co* v *Shand & Co* (6).

In a cif contract the seller is usually required to furnish the buyer with a notice of appropriation. If so, the seller must comply with the contractual time for providing it. Provided it is given in time, and contains the necessary details, it will be a valid notice of appropriation and cannot be withdrawn: *Grain Union SA Antwerp* v *Hans Larsen Aalborg SA* (7). This has sometimes had the result that the seller cannot perform the contract.

The decisions in these cases have show the courts' view that commercial contracts require more certainty. It is, therefore, necessary to have strict rules as to the time for performing the various stages of the contracts. Unfortunately, if the time stipulation is not adhered to, it does allow the other party to the contract to treat the non-compliance as a repudiatory breach. This has resulted in the cancellation of a contract for what would seem to the lay person to be a minor breach; for example, where a notice of loading was given by the 17th of the month instead of the 15th: *Gill & Duffus SA* v *Société pour l'Exportation des Sucres* (8). Obviously, the 'innocent' party may waive the breach, but it is possible for, say, a buyer to use what would sometimes appear to be a technicality to cancel the contract. Whether a party waives a breach, or uses it to cancel the contract, will sometimes depend on the market price of the goods. Some contracts do permit a degree of flexibility by inserting 'within a reasonable time'; or the courts may, in fact, find a 'reasonable time' implied into the contract: *The Naxos* (9).

b) The doctrine of strict compliance and the autonomy of credit are two underlying principles of the letter of credit. Both principles are strictly adhered to by the courts who are loath to undermine the security of letters of credit and international trade.

The doctrine of strict compliance means that the documents tendered by the beneficiary to the buyer's bank must comply exactly with the terms of the credit. Documents which are almost correct are not good enough and should be rejected by the bank: *Equitable Trust Co of New York* v *Dawson* (10). If the bank accepts incorrect documents, it will not be entitled to reimbursement by the buyer. If the bank wishes to be reimbursed, it must follow the instructions of the applicant: *J H Rayner & Oilseeds Trading Co Ltd* v *Hambros Bank Ltd* (11). In that case the bank was entitled to reject documents which referred to 'machine-shelled groundnut kernels' instead of 'coromandels' as required under the terms of the credit. The two descriptions refer to the same goods, but the bank's rejection was upheld by the Court of Appeal. The bank is not concerned whether the applicant's instructions are reasonable or unreasonable. To decide otherwise would require the bank to go beyond looking at the face of the documents but instead to go behind them. This is contrary to arts 13 and 15 of the Uniform Customs and Practice for Documentary Credits (UCP) (No 500, 1993 Revision). Article 13 states that the bank is under a duty to take reasonable care in determining whether the documents presented by the beneficiary are in accordance with the terms of the credit. The bank has a reasonable time (not to exceed seven banking days) in which to decide whether to accept or reject the documents. If the bank accepts the documents, it is not stating that the documents are genuine or authentic: art 15. The banks would be put in an impossible position if they had to check the authenticity of documents, or even to check trade terms as in the *Rayner* case.

If the UCP articles are incorporated into the credit, they mitigate some of the rigours of the common law. Article 39 of the UCP allows for a tolerance level when dealing with any quantity other than individual items. Following the doctrine of strict compliance, the court in *Moralice Ltd* v *E D & F Mann* (12) stated that the de minimus rule did not apply to letters of credit. Yet, both the common law and the UCP allow for a general description of the goods in documents other than the commercial invoice: *Soproma SpA* v *Marine and Animal By-Products Corporation* (13); art 37(c) UCP. But, generally, the courts will adhere to the doctrine of strict compliance in order not to undermine international trade.

The other principle which is at the heart of the letter of credit is the autonomy of the credit. This principle provides that the letter of credit once opened is separate from the underlying sales contract. The parties deal in documents and not in goods: arts 3 and 4 UCP. The confirmed irrevocable credit is a guarantee of payment to the beneficiary, usually the seller under the sales contract, and it cannot be amended or cancelled without the consent of all parties, including the beneficiary: art 9 UCP. This principle applies even if there is a dispute on the sales contract: *Hamzeh Malas* v *British Imex Industries Ltd* (14). In that case the Court of Appeal said that it would be wrong to interfere with the established practice that a confirmed letter of credit imposed upon the bank an absolute obligation to pay irrespective of any dispute on the sales contract.

If the correct documents are presented by the beneficiary, and the terms of the credit are complied with, the only situation which can prevent payment under a confirmed irrevocable letter of credit is if there is fraud by the beneficiary: *United City Merchants (Investments) Ltd* v *Royal Bank of Canada* (15). An allegation of fraud will not be sufficient to stop payment (*Discount Records Ltd* v *Barclays Bank Ltd* (16)), neither will established fraud by someone other than the beneficiary: *United City Merchants*.

However, in *Tukan Timber* v *Barclays Bank plc* (17) the court did raise the concern that in the interests of international commerce the letters of credit should not be able to be used for the purposes of fraud. In that case a comparison was made with the United States of America where interlocutory relief is more readily obtainable. However, *United City Merchants*, a House of Lords decision, is still good law.

In conclusion, therefore, the doctrines of strict compliance and the autonomy of the credit are still the underlying principles of the letter of credit. They shall remain so whilst courts are reluctant to interfere with established commercial practice.

References

(1) [1981] 2 All ER 540
(2) [1954] 2 QB 402
(3) [1975] 2 Lloyd's Rep 235
(4) [1952] 1 Lloyd's Rep 183
(5) [1965] 2 Lloyd's Rep 757
(6) (1877) 2 App Cas 455
(7) (1933) 150 LT 78
(8) [1985] 1 Lloyd's Rep 621
(9) [1990] 1 WLR 1337
(10) (1927) 27 Ll LR 49
(11) [1943] 1 KB 37
(12) [1954] 2 Lloyd's Rep 526
(13) [1966] 1 Lloyd's Rep 367
(14) [1958] 2 QB 127
(15) [1982] 2 WLR 1039
(16) [1975] 1 All ER 1071
(17) [1987] 1 QB 171

QUESTION 5

BSH plc are suppliers of office equipment. They have recently encountered a number of problems with customers in connection with the following contracts and they seek your advice.

a) BSH sold a computer to Jack, a self-employed accountant, who bought the computer both for use in his business and for use by his children. The screen of the computer has a thin scratch running across it but the scratch does not affect the operation of the computer in any way. Jack claims that he is entitled to reject the computer. The price of the computer has dropped sharply on the market.

b) BSH supplied two chairs to Susan, a self-employed estate agent. Susan claims that the fabric on the back of the chair has caused her to contract a rare skin infection and she has now been off work for a number of weeks. The other chair was used by Anne, a secretary whom Susan employed on a part-time basis. Last week the chair suddenly gave way when Anne was sitting on it and Anne suffered extensive injuries in the fall.

c) BSH sold a photocopier to Xerxes plc. The contract stated that:

> 'To remedy defects the purchaser shall allow the supplier the time and opportunity required as estimated by the supplier. Should the purchaser refuse to allow such time and opportunity, the supplier shall be released from the obligations to remedy the defects. The purchaser shall return the defective goods at his own expense to the supplier immediately upon request of the latter. All other warranties or conditions are hereby expressly excluded.'

Yugo, the managing director of Xerxes, claims that the photocopier is defective but he refuses to return the photocopier for repair because he claims that a local supplier can carry out the repairs effectively and he wishes to recover the cost of repair from BSH. Alternatively, he claims that, if he is obliged by the terms of the contract to return the goods to BSH, Xerxes cannot be made to pay for the cost of returning the photocopier to BSH.

SUGGESTED SOLUTION TO QUESTION 5

General Comment

This should be a popular question. Part (a) raises the issues of satisfactory quality under s14(2) Sale of Goods Act (SGA) 1979 and the right to reject subject to s15A SGA 1979. Part (b) requires a discussion of s14(3) SGA 1979 and cases such as *Griffiths* v *Peter Conway Ltd*, whereas Anne's claim would be brought under the Consumer Protection Act 1987. Part (c) raises the issue of exclusion clauses and the Unfair Contract Terms Act 1977.

Skeleton Solution

a) Section 14(2) SGA 1979.
   'Appearance and finish'.
   Section 15A SGA 1979.
   'Dealing as a consumer'.

b) Section 14(3) SGA 1979.
   Griffiths v *Peter Conway Ltd.*
   Consumer Protection Act 1987.
   Status of BSH under the CPA 1987.

c) Exclusion clause.
   Section 6(3) Unfair Contract Terms Act 1977.
   Reasonableness and incorporation.
   Right to reject subject and acceptance.

Suggested Solution

a) Jack may be able to reject the computer sold to him by BSH plc if there is a breach of s14(2) Sale of Goods Act (SGA) 1979.

   Section 14(2) (amended by the Sale and Supply of Goods Act 1994) states that if goods are sold in the course of business there is an implied term, which is a condition, that the goods will be of satisfactory quality. Satisfactory quality is defined as the standard that a reasonable person would regard as satisfactory taking into account the description, the price (if relevant) and other relevant circumstances: s14(2) SGA 1979. The implied condition does not apply to defects brought to the attention of the buyer or to defects which could be discovered by the buyer on a reasonable examination.

Section 14(2A) give a list of factors which can be taken into account in determining whether goods are of satisfactory quality. The list includes 'appearance and finish'. In *Rogers* v *Parish (Scarborough) Ltd* (1) the Court held that the appearance of a car could be taken into account in determining whether it was of merchantable quality (the test prior to satisfactory quality).

Jack may, therefore, have an argument for rejecting the computer, subject to acceptance after a reasonable opportunity to examine the goods: s35 SGA 1979. However, Jack is a self-employed accountant who bought the computer for use in his business and for use by his children. Under s15A SGA 1979 (inserted by the Sale and Supply of Goods Act 1994) a buyer who is not dealing as a consumer may not be able to reject goods if the breach of the implied terms – ss13, 14 or 15 SGA 1979 – is so slight that it would be unreasonable to reject. It is for the seller, BSH plc, to show that s15A applies to the situation.

'Dealing as a consumer' is defined in s12 Unfair Contract Terms Act 1977 as someone who is not buying in the course of business, buys from someone who is selling in the course of business, and the goods are of a type ordinarily supplied for private use or consumption. It may well be argued that Jack's purchase of the computer is a one-off transaction which is not an integral part of his business. If that is the case, Jack will be dealing as a consumer and s15A SGA 1979 will not be applicable: *R & B Customs Brokers Co Ltd* v *United Dominions Trust Ltd* (2).

b) Susan will want to bring a claim against BSH plc for the injury that she has suffered as a result of using the chair. If the goods are sold in the course of business there is an implied condition that the goods will be fit for their purpose if that purpose has been made known to the seller and the buyer has reasonably relied on the skill and experience of the seller: s14(3) SGA 1979. It has been held that when certain goods are bought, the seller will know by implication the purpose for which they have been bought: *Priest* v *Last* (3)

In *Griffiths* v *Peter Conway Ltd* (4), when a buyer of a tweed coat contracted a skin infection, it was held that the buyer should have informed the seller of her skin condition. Similarly, Susan should have informed BSH plc of any skin condition which may react badly to particular types of fabric. It is, therefore, unlikely that Susan would be able to reject the chair and claim in damages against BSH plc for breach of s14(3) SGA 1979. Of course, if the fabric would have affected someone with average skin, there may well be a breach of s14(3). If Susan does have a claim against BSH plc, the fact that she may not be dealing as a consumer would not prevent her rejecting the chair as presumably the breach is not so slight as to make s15A applicable.

The second chair has caused Anne injuries. Anne would not have a claim against BSH plc under the Sale of Goods Act 1979 because she did not buy the chair. However, Anne would have a possible claim against BSH plc under the Consumer Protection Act (CPA) 1987.

Under the CPA 1987 a manufacturer, an importer into the EU or an own-brander can be made liable for injuries caused by defective products: s2 CPA 1987. A supplier may also be liable if the supplier fails to identify one of the parties listed in s2 CPA 1987.

The defect must have existed at the time the product was supplied and, unless Anne was using the chair in an unusual manner, it would seem that there is no defence for BSH plc under s4 CPA 1987. Anne may claim damages for her injuries, although Susan would not be able to recover for damage to the chair itself: s5 CPA 1987.

c) The clause in the contract between BSH plc and Xerxes plc is attempting to exclude liability for breach of the implied terms, ie ss13–15 SGA 1979. The implied terms cannot be excluded in a consumer sale and may only be excluded in a non-consumer sale if the exclusion clause is reasonable: s6(3) Unfair Contract Terms Act (UCTA) 1977.

If Xerxes plc is buying in the course of business and, therefore, not dealing as a consumer (s12 UCTA 1977), the clause attempting to exclude liability would have to be incorporated into the contract and be reasonable: s6(3) UCTA 1977. When determining whether the clause is reasonable, the courts will take into account the bargaining strengths of the parties and whether the party bound by it in reality consented to the inserting of such a clause.

In *AEG (UK) Ltd* v *Logic Resource Ltd* (5) Hobhouse LJ held that a similar clause amounted to giving a limited warranty cover and the last sentence of the clause was an exclusion clause. The clause was incorporated into the contract following *Parker* v *South Eastern Railway Co* (6), but the party attempting to rely on the clause had failed to satisfy the burden of showing that the other party to the contract in reality consented to the clause.

If the clause is not upheld, Xerxes plc may be able to reject the goods if there is a breach of s14(2) or (3) SGA 1979. The right to reject is subject to Xerxes plc having accepted the photocopier. If the photocopier is repaired by the seller, or under an arrangement with the seller, that will not be seen as acceptance: s35(6) SGA 1979. If Xerxes gets a local supplier to repair the photocopier, it may be seen as acceptance.

Unless the court hold Xerxes plc bound by the contract term to return the photocopier to BSH plc, Xerxes is only required to make it available at the contractual place of examination which may be Xerxes' place of business.

References

(1) [1987] 2 WLR 353
(2) [1988] 1 All ER 847
(3) [1903] 2 KB 148
(4) [1939] 1 All ER 685
(5) [1996] CLC 265
(6) (1877) 2 CPD 416

QUESTION 6

a) Albert has 1,000 bottles of wine in his warehouse. He agreed to sell 200 bottles each to Brian, Cedric, Donald and Evelina and 100 bottles each to Frank and Gerald. All but Gerald paid Albert in advance. Under the terms of the contracts of sale Albert agreed to supply the stipulated quantities of wine from his warehouse, but he reserved the right to supply wine of the same quality from another source in the event of a shortfall for whatever reason of the stocks in his warehouse. Albert is now insolvent but he has not supplied any of his purchasers with their wine.

Advise the purchasers. What difference would it make to your answer if Frank, Brian and Cedric had taken delivery of their wine prior to the insolvency of Albert and it is now discovered that there are only 300 bottles of wine in the warehouse?

b) Pablo, a Spanish wine merchant, agreed to sell 5,000 bottles of sherry to Albert fob Bilbao. Pablo entered into a contract with Picasso Ltd for the carriage of the sherry on board the vessel *Enterprise*. After the sherry had been loaded onto the *Enterprise*, but before it reaches London, Pablo is told that Albert is bankrupt and that he will not be able to pay for the goods. He has also been told that some of the sherry has been damaged as a result of being stowed on deck rather than below deck. The contract of carriage was silent on the point whether the goods must be stowed above deck or below deck.

Advise Pablo.

SUGGESTED SOLUTION TO QUESTION 6

General Comment

Part (a) raised the issue of unascertained goods and ss20A and 20B of the Sale of Goods Act 1979. Part (b) required a discussion of the unpaid seller's right of stoppage in transit, and a shipper's claim against the carrier in respect of damage to goods during transit.

Skeleton Solution

a) Unascertained goods.

   Sections 20A and 20B Sale of Goods Act 1979.

   Re Wait.

b) Fob contract: passing of risk.

   Unpaid seller's right of stoppage in transit.

   Carrier's obligation to care for cargo.

   Possible quasi-deviation point.

Suggested Solution

a) Albert agreed to sell to a number of buyers bottles of wine which at the time of the contract were unascertained goods. Albert is now insolvent and the purchasers' rights, if any, will depend on whether they have any interest in the subject-matter.

   Section 16 Sale of Goods Act (SGA) 1979 requires goods to be ascertained before property in the goods can pass to the buyer. However, s16 is now subject to s20A SGA 1979 (which was inserted by by Sale of Goods (Amendment) Act 1995).

   Section 20A states that on payment of the price of the goods, a buyer of a specified quantity from an identifiable bulk will have common ownership in the bulk cargo. This amendment to the SGA 1979 was designed to deal with the problem which arose in *Re Wait* (1). In that case, the buyer had paid for a quantity of wheat which at the time of the contact was unascertained. The seller became insolvent and the buyer wished to claim the wheat. It was held that the buyer had no rights in the goods because property had not passed to the buyer.

   We are told that all the purchasers except Gerald have paid in advance for the bottles of wine. Accordingly, the purchasers should be able to claim common ownership in the bottles of wine. However, Albert has reserved the right to supply wine from another source in the event of a shortfall. This term of the contract may prevent s20A applying to our situation because it could be argued that there will not be an identifiable bulk from which the bottles of wine are to be supplied. If s20A does not apply to our situation, the purchasers who have paid in advance will not be able to claim the goods, but will instead be creditors in liquidation: *Re Wait*.

If s20A does apply, despite the term in the contract allowing Albert to supply wine from another source, the purchasers who have paid in advance are deemed to have consented to dealing in the goods: s20B SGA 1979. In which case, if Frank, Brian and Cedric had taken delivery of their wine prior to the insolvency of Albert, they are not under a duty to compensate the remaining purchasers, Donald and Evelina. Donald and Evelina will have their share of the wine reduced proportionately (s20A(4) SGA 1979) and will be creditors in liquidation for the amount which has been paid and for which they have received no delivery of wine.

Gerald did not pay in advance for the supply of wine and, therefore, his position will be unaffected by s20A SGA 1979. Gerald will not be able to claim the bottles of wine but will have a claim against Albert for non-delivery of the wine. Since Albert is in liquidation, Gerald is unlikely to have any remedy.

b) Under a fob contract property and risk usually pass on shipment: *Inglis* v *Stock* (2). This, of course, is always subject to the intention of the parties: *Mitsui & Co Ltd* v *Flota Mercante Grancolombiana SA* (3).

When Pablo is informed that Albert is bankrupt and will not be able to pay for the goods, Pablo would be able to exercise the unpaid seller's right of stoppage in transit: s44 SGA 1979. Pablo would also have the right of resale which would rescind the original contract, but would still allow him to claim the difference between the market price and the original contract price from Albert: s48 SGA 1979; *R V Ward Ltd* v *Bignall* (4). Obviously this last right is unlikely to be of much use to Pablo in the light of Albert's insolvency.

Some of the sherry has been damaged as a result of being stowed on deck. A carrier is under a duty to look after the goods and to deliver them in the condition in which they were shipped. The obligation applies at both common law and under the Hague-Visby Rules, which have been implemented into English law by the Carriage of Goods by Sea Act 1979. The question is silent as to whether a bill of lading has been issued in respect of the goods and, if it has, whether it contains a clause stating that the Rules apply or that English law governs the contract. (Spain is not a Contracting State to the Hague-Visby Rules.) In the absence of the bill of lading and the required clause if, from the circumstances, English law applies to the contract of carriage, Pablo would have a claim against the carrier based on a breach of the common law duty to look after the cargo. This duty of care includes proper stowage: *Elder Dempster* v *Paterson Zochonis* (5). The fact that the goods have been stowed on deck when the contract of carriage did not refer to deck cargo may amount to a quasi-deviation. If that is the case, it is debatable whether the carrier would be able to rely on any excepted perils contained in the contract of carriage: *Kenya Railways* v *Antares Co Pte Ltd, The Antares* (6). From the facts it appears that Pablo would have a good claim for damages based on the carrier's breach of contract.

References

(1) [1927] 1 Ch 606
(2) (1885) 10 App Cas 263
(3) [1989] 1 All ER 951
(4) [1967] 1 QB 534
(5) [1924] All ER 135
(6) [1987] 1 Lloyd's Rep 424

QUESTION 7

a) Critically evaluate section 24 of the Sale of Goods Act 1979. Should the section be reformed? If so, how?

b) Lotty Leather plc entered into a contract with Sharp Shoes Ltd under which Lotty agreed to supply Sharp with 'all its requirements for leather in the manufacture of shoes'. A further term of the contract stated that ownership of the leather was to remain with Lotty until payment had been made in full under all orders. While Sharp were given authority to sell any goods which had been made with leather supplied by Lotty, they could only do so if they entered into any such sales contracts as agents for Lotty and they paid all the proceeds of sale over to Lotty without delay. Sharp is now insolvent. Leather to the value of £7,000 has been found in Sharp's factory. Some of the leather has been cut. There are also shoes worth £12,000 in the factory and Sharp has entered into a number of contracts 'as agent for Lotty Leather' under which the customers remain liable to pay £12,000. Sharp owe Lotty Leather £30,000.

Advise Lotty Leather.

SUGGESTED SOLUTION TO QUESTION 7

General Comment

This question should not have caused many problems for students. It is a fairly standard question. Part (a) dealt with one of the exceptions to the nemo dat rule, namely s24 Sale of Goods Act 1979. Part (b) required a discussion of retention of title clauses.

Skeleton Solution

a) Nemo dat rule.
   Section 24 Sale of Goods Act 1979.
   Pacific Motor Auctions Pty Ltd.
   Worcester Works Finance Ltd.

b) Retention of title clause: s19 Sale of Goods Act 1979.
   'All monies' clause.
   Mixed goods; book debts.
   Floating charge.

Suggested Solution

a) Section 24 Sale of Goods Act (SGA) 1979 is one of the exceptions to the nemo dat rule contained in s21 SGA 1979. Section 21 provides that a buyer will not get good title if the seller of the goods is not the owner or did not have the authority or consent of the owner to sell the goods. This will be subject to the owner of the goods being precluded by conduct from denying that the seller had authority to sell: s21(1) SGA 1979.

   Section 24 of the Act states that if a seller continues or is in possession of the goods or documents of title after sale, then if the seller delivers the goods or documents of title to another under a sale or other disposition, the second buyer receiving the goods or documents of title in good faith and without notice of the previous sale will acquire a good title. Section 24 SGA 1979 is similar in wording to s8 Factors Act 1889.

   In order for s24 SGA 1979 to apply, the seller must have be in possession of the goods or documents of title at the time of the second sale or disposition. The section refers to 'continues or is in possession'. If a seller's possession is that of a bailee, for example where the seller has hired back the goods under an agreement with the original buyer, s24 is still applicable: *Pacific*

Motor Auctions Pty v *Motor Credits Ltd* (1). In that case the Privy Council stated that the seller does not have to remain in possession of the goods as a seller; all that is required is that there is continuity of possession. The decision in *Pacific Motor Auctions Pty* v *Motor Credits Ltd* was followed by the Court of Appeal in *Worcester Works Finance Ltd* v *Cooden Engineering Co Ltd* (2).

As far as the words 'or other disposition' in s24 SGA 1979 is concerned, the Court of Appeal in *Worcester Works Finance Ltd* v *Cooden Engineering Co Ltd* held that they should be given a wide interpretation. In that case the seller sold and delivered a car to the buyer, who in turn sold the car to a finance company, but the original buyer retained possession of the car. The original seller repossessed the car because the buyer's cheque was dishonoured. The finance company sued the original seller for the car. It was held that the repossession by the original seller amounted to 'disposition' for the purpose of s24 SGA 1979 and, accordingly, property in the car had re-vested in the original seller.

The second buyer, in order to get good title under s24 SGA 1979, must act in good faith and without notice of the original contract of sale. Such good faith must exist at the date of the second contract and at the date of delivery of the goods or documents of title to the second buyer.

It may be argued that s24 SGA 1979 should be reformed to ensure that it is not used in a situation such as that found in *Worcester Works Finance Ltd* v *Cooden Engineering Co Ltd*. The section should operate to protect the innocent purchaser. The term 'disposition' should, therefore, be defined by statute and be given a narrow meaning.

b) Lotty Leather's rights depend on whether the reservation of title clause in the contract will be upheld by the courts.

A seller of goods may reserve the right of disposal until some condition has been fulfilled, for example until full payment has been made: s19 SGA 1979.

A simple retention of title clause, often referred to as a Romalpa clause, is not registrable under the Companies Act 1985. However, the clause in the contract with Sharp Shoes goes beyond being a simple retention of title clause. Lotty Leather is attempting to reserve ownership in leather supplied until payment has been made in full under all orders. This type of 'all monies' clause was upheld by the House of Lords in *Armour* v *Thyssen Edelstahlwerke AG* (3).

A problem arises when dealing with the goods which have been used and the proceeds of sale. If goods have become mixed with other goods, the seller cannot retain legal title in the new goods: *Clough Mill Ltd* v *Martin* (4), and *Re Peachdart Ltd* (5). In these circumstances the courts have held that the buyer is in fact creating a floating charge over the assets in favour of the seller: *Borden (UK)* v *Scottish Timber Products Ltd* (6). A floating charge requires registration under s396 Companies Act 1985.

The shoes worth £12,000 presumably have been made using leather supplied by Lotty Leather. A charge has, therefore, been created in favour of Lotty Leather and will be void as against the liquidator if it is not registered. As far as the leather which had been cut, it is still identifiable as the leather supplied under the contract. If that is so, Lotty Leather would be able to reclaim the leather, although, of course, it is subject to the leather now being of any use to Lotty Leather.

Regarding the contracts which Sharp entered into 'as agent for Lotty Leather', in *Aluminium Industrie Vaassen BV* v *Romalpa Aluminium Ltd* (7) much of the discussion centred on the existence of a fiduciary relationship between the seller and the buyer. In that case it was held that the seller had an equitable right to trace the proceeds of sale. The *Romalpa* decision has been criticised and courts today tend to distinguish it. In *Re Bond Worth* (8) a similar clause was held to amount to reserving equitable title to the seller. As such, the clause would be creating a floating charge over the company's book debts and would, therefore, need to be registered under the Companies Act 1905: *Compaq Computer Ltd* v *Abercorn Group Ltd* (9). If the floating charges are not registered, they are void as against other creditors and the liquidator. Lotty Leather would then be an unsecured creditor in liquidation for the amount owed under the contracts.

References

(1) [1965] AC 867
(2) [1972] 1 QB 210
(3) [1991] 2 AC 339
(4) [1985] 1 WLR 111
(5) [1984] Ch 131
(6) [1981] Ch 25
(7) [1976] 1 WLR 676
(8) [1980] Ch 228
(9) [1993] BCLC 603

QUESTION 8

Martin is the manager of the Red Dwarf Hotel. The hotel is owned by Crust plc. It is a term of Martin's contract that he must not, without the authority of the managing director of Crust, place an order for goods worth more than £10,000. Martin is also expressly forbidden from ordering any alcohol because all alcohol is supplied to the hotel directly by Crust. Nora, a sales representative of Prosper Foods, visits Martin and persuades him that it makes good business sense to order his food in bulk and that Prosper has special discounts on all orders over £15,000. Martin informs Nora that he needs the authority of his managing director to place an order in excess of £10,000. While Nora is in his office, Martin picks up the phone and pretends to hold a conversation with his managing director in which he appears to obtain the permission of his managing director to enter into the transaction (in fact he was talking to his girlfriend, Roberta). Martin then signs a contract to order food to the value of £17,000 in his own name. Nora also persuades Martin to enter into a contract to purchase £5,000 worth of alcohol by offering to give him 100 free cigars.

The hotel is rather run down and requires redecoration. Martin has received from a local firm a quotation of £12,000 for the work. He decides that his two brothers could do the job more cheaply. They work for a small company, of which Martin is also a director. Martin enters into an agreement with his brother under which he agrees to pay them £9,800 and to provide them and their families with free meals for a year if they carry out the redecoration work. They agree. The redecoration has now been done and Prosper has delivered the food and alcohol to the Red Dwarf Hotel. The managing director of Crust, having discovered the above facts, is refusing to pay either Martin's brothers or Prosper and is threatening to dismiss Martin.

Discuss.

SUGGESTED SOLUTION TO QUESTION 8

General Comment

If students have covered agency as part of their revision, this should have been a popular question. It deals with the relationships between the parties: principal and agent; principal and third party; and agent and third party. The only problem would occur in knowing when to stop!

Skeleton Solution

Types of authority.

Representations to a third party.

Agent's liability on a contract.

Fiduciary duties of an agent.

Suggested Solution

The rights and liabilities of the various parties will depend on whether Martin has acted within his authority as an agent of Crust. A principal will be bound by the acts of an agent who is acting within his/her authority.

Martin, as manager of the Red Dwarf Hotel, has had limits placed on his actual authority in that under the terms of his contract he must not enter into certain contracts on behalf of the hotel. However, Martin as a manager will also have usual or apparent authority. Usual authority is the authority given to someone in a particular position, ie it is the type of authority which comes with the post. Apparent authority is the type of authority which the principal has held the agent out as possessing. The representation may be made by the principal in giving the agent a position in which he/she would have usual authority to enter into certain transactions, for example the appointment of Martin to manager of the hotel.

With regard to the first contract, the order for food to the value of £17,000, Martin has acted outside of his actual authority which was limited to placing orders for food up to £10,000. However, Crust will still be bound by the contract if Martin has acted within his usual or apparent authority. In *Armagas Ltd* v *Mundogas SA, The Ocean Frost* (1) the third party to a contract for the hire of a ship knew that generally the agent did not have authority to enter into this particular contract. But the agent claimed that he had been given the specific authority necessary for the transaction. The House of Lords held that as the third party knew that the agent generally had no authority to enter into such a transaction, the agent by representing himself that he had specific authority on this one occasion could not bind the principal. This case would, therefore, suggest that Martin could not bind Crust on the order for food. However, if *First Energy Ltd* v *Hungarian International Bank Ltd* (2) is followed then Crust may be bound by the contract. In *First Energy* the third party knew that the agent had no authority to enter into a particular transaction, but also knew that the agent's head office was where the decisions were made. The Court of Appeal held that the agent had apparent authority to communicate decisions made by the head office. The principal was, therefore, bound by the transaction when the third party reasonably relied on the agent's statement that the principal had given him authority to enter into the transaction.

Whether Prosper, using *First Energy*, can bind Crust to the contract will depend to some extent on whether it was reasonable for Prosper to accept Martin's statement that he had been given the authority to make the contract.

Martin has also entered into a contract to purchase £5,000 worth of alcohol despite orders to the contrary. Martin is, therefore, acting outside of his actual authority. As regards his usual or apparent authority, it may be argued that a manager usually has the authority to order alcohol for the hotel. However, the fact that Nora has persuaded Martin to enter into the contract by offering him 100 free cigars suggests that Nora was aware of Martin's lack of authority.

If Crust is not liable on the contracts for the food and alcohol, Prosper may have a claim against Martin based on breach of warranty of authority: *Collen* v *Wright* (3). If Crust is bound by the contract for the food, Martin may still be a party to that contract because he has signed the contract in his own name. In order to avoid liability Martin should have made it clear that he was signing as a representative of the principal: *Punjab National Bank* v *De Boinville* (4).

An agent has fiduciary duties to his/her principal. An agent is under a duty to avoid a conflict of interest and is under a duty not to take a bribe. Martin has been offered 100 free cigars in return for entering into the contract to purchase alcohol, and he has entered into an agreement with his brothers whereby they will undertake the redecoration.

A bribe may be any type of inducement which is kept secret from the principal: *Anangel Atlas Compania Naviera SA* v *Ishikawajima-Harima Heavy Industries Ltd* (5). On finding out about the bribe Crust may dismiss Martin without notice and rescind the contract with Prosper. If Crust rescinds the contract, it is unlikely that there has been any loss caused by the bribe and, therefore, Crust will not have an action in the tort of deceit.

The hotel required redecoration and, in fact, the brothers' quote of £9,800 is less than the local firm's quote of £12,000, although free meals for a year could substantially increase the cost of the redecoration work. Apart from the fact that it is his brothers who carried out the redecoration work, Martin is a director of their company. However, even if Crust has benefited from the transaction, Martin is still in breach of his fiduciary duty not to put himself in a position where there is a conflict of interest: *Boardman* v *Phipps* (6). Martin may be liable for any profit he has made as a result of the transaction. If the brothers knew that Martin was acting outside the scope of his authority they would not be able to enforce the contract. If Martin represented that he had the authority to enter into the contract, he may be liable to their company for breach of warranty of authority (see discussion above).

References

(1) [1986] 2 All ER 385
(2) [1993] 2 Lloyd's Rep 194
(3) (1857) 8 E & B 647
(4) [1992] 3 All ER 104
(5) [1990 1 Lloyd's Rep 167
(6) [1967] 2 AC 46

Old Bailey Press

The Old Bailey Press integrated student library is planned and written to help you at every stage of your studies. Each of our range of Textbooks, Casebooks, Revision WorkBooks and Statutes are all designed to work together and are regularly revised and updated.

We are also able to offer you Suggested Solutions which provide you with past examination questions and solutions for most of the subject areas listed below.

You can buy Old Bailey Press books from your University Bookshop or your local Bookshop, or in case of difficulty, order direct using this form.

Here is the selection of modules covered by our series:

Administrative Law; Commercial Law; Company Law (no Single Paper 1997); Conflict of Laws (no Suggested Solutions Pack); Constitutional Law: The Machinery of Government; Obligations: Contract Law; Conveyancing (no Revision Workbook); Criminology (Sourcebook in place of a Casebook or Revision WorkBook); Criminal Law; English Legal System; Equity and Trusts; Law of The European Union; Evidence; Family Law; Jurisprudence: The Philosophy of Law (Sourcebook in place of a Casebook); Land: The Law of Real Property; Law of International Trade; Legal Skills and System (Textbook only); Public International Law; Revenue Law (no Casebook); Succession: The Law of Wills and Estates; Obligations: The Law of Tort.

Mail order prices:

Textbook £11.95

Casebook £9.95

Revision WorkBook £7.95

Statutes £9.95

Suggested Solutions Pack (1991–1995) £6.95

Single Paper 1996 £3.00

Single Paper 1997 £3.00

To complete your order, please fill in the form below:

Module	Books required	Quantity	Price	Cost
		Postage		
		TOTAL		

For Europe, add 15% postage and packing (£20 maximum).
For the rest of the world, add 40% for airmail.

ORDERING

By telephone to Mail Order at 020 7385 3377, with your credit card to hand.

By fax to 020 7381 3377 (giving your credit card details).

By post to:

Old Bailey Press, 200 Greyhound Road, London W14 9RY.

When ordering by post, please enclose full payment by cheque or banker's draft, or complete the credit card details below.

We aim to despatch your books within 3 working days of receiving your order.

Name

Address

Postcode Telephone

Total value of order, including postage: £

I enclose a cheque/banker's draft for the above sum, or

charge my ☐ Access/Mastercard ☐ Visa ☐ American Express

Card number

☐☐☐☐ ☐☐☐☐ ☐☐☐☐ ☐☐☐☐

Expiry date ☐☐☐☐

Signature: ....Date: ....